North West Steamships

Edward Paget-Tomlinson

The Isle of Man paddle steamer *Mona's Queen* at Whitehaven. *(Whitehaven Museum).*

Acknowledgements

Most works of this kind are compilations, impossible to achieve without a great deal of help from numerous people. Illustrations are individually credited, but the author would like to thank all the under-mentioned for the information they gave, additional to the supply of pictures. The text would never have been finished if they had not come to the rescue: W. G. Baillie, Fleetwood; David Buckley, Fleetwood; George Carter, Fleetwood; John Clarkson, Preston; Harry Fancy, Whitehaven Museum; W. B. Hallam, Liverpool; David Hughes and Bryn Trescathric, Furness Museum; Keith Ingham, Lancaster; Alan Lockett, Barrow-in-Furness; Mrs Diana Matthews, Windermere Nautical Trust; Trevor Morgan, Seascale; Alan Pearsall, Morecambe; Joseph Price, Ulverston; Miss Annie S. Robinson, M.B.E. J.P., Maryport; K. E. Royall, Barrow-in-Furness; Raymond Sankey, Barrow-in-Furness; James Sawbridge, Lytham St. Anne's; Michael Walker, Heysham; Jonathan Wignall, Barrow-in-Furness; Keith Willacy, Morecambe; John Wilson, Ulverston; Malcolm Wilson, Silloth.

In addition I would like to thank library staffs at Barrow-in-Furness, Fleetwood, in particular Catherine Rothwell, Kendal, Maryport, Preston and Workington, also the Ullswater Navigation and Transit Co. Ltd., and Mrs Jennifer Snell and Mrs Ann Sweeney who between them tackled all the typing, a daunting task. Finally I would like to thank Douglas Moreton of Countryside Publications for all his patience, in handling the manuscript and seeing it through publication.

Published by Countryside Publications Limited, School Lane, Brinscall, Chorley, Lancashire.

Text© Edward Paget-Tomlinson, 1980

Printed by Tamley-Reed Limited.

ISBN 0 86157 039 1

Introduction

Steam entered the commercial shipping scene at the end of the Napoleonic Wars and grew more dominant as the nineteenth century advanced, although sail remained competitive in certain trades well into the twentieth century. Steam power however has died very suddenly, since the Second World War, eclipsed by the diesel, economical both in space and fuel. Today steam has joined sail in history, so that an illustrated book like this can be written with strong nostalgic appeal, unthinkable in the 1930s, and hardly credible in the 1950s.

Some motor vessels appear in the following pages to round off the story, but the main interest is the coal fired reciprocating engined steamer, screw or paddle. Geographically the survey starts up in the Solway and ends at the Ribble, the top north west corner of England. To include Liverpool and the Mersey ports would have thrown the whole work out of balance, it is a local study and within these geographical limits, the various types of powered vessel are described.

Very early steamers were limited in their usefulness, to short range tasks in sheltered waters, for example passenger services on the Clyde. In north-west England steamships were operating coastal services between Lancaster and Liverpool as early as the 1820s, by which time they had become more venturesome. A steamer, in spite of weak boilers and uncertain machinery, could offer reliable schedules which a sailing ship could not match, and such coastal operations as those between Lancaster and Liverpool quickly spread to the ports further north, including by about 1825 Port Carlisle on the Solway, the entrance to the Carlisle Canal. There was at this time no competition from road transport, limited to horse power, and none yet from the infant railways, still to be linked into a system. For their part the rivers and canals looked on the sea as the outlet for their traffic, indeed many of the navigation companies owned ships, for example the Lancaster Canal.

Steamers did have the disadvantage of excessive fuel consumption, which meant that much of their under deck space was taken up with bunkers. For this reason they could carry little cargo, so most of them concentrated on passengers with stowage space for parcels and high value goods. A mail contract was a godsend to the early operators, indeed the post office subsidy was frequently essential to pay for the high cost of operation. So the passenger and mail steam packets rapidly gained ascendancy and their design advanced as competition grew stronger. Most of the services to Ireland and the Isle of Man ran from Liverpool, but the railway system offered a chance to other ports. Indeed it was the competition between rival railway companies to establish steamship lines which created the multifarious routes of the nineteenth century, serving Ireland and the Continent. The railways created their own ports, Fleetwood and Heysham are north west examples, and their ships became faster and more comfortable, at least for the first class, as the century advanced. Certain shipyards, for example Denny's of Dumbarton, concentrated on railway steamer building, and took advantage of every technical innovation. Thus the steam turbine was early applied, to the Midland Railway's *Londonderry* and *'Manxman* in 1904.

Excursion steamers, in the days before the motor car, were immensely popular. They worked between rail served ports so that round trips were possible, and had a particular advantage in the Morecambe Bay area where land communications have always been difficult. Barrow and Blackpool are not far apart by sea, some 22 miles, but by land 65. Fleetwood, Morecambe, and even Grange-over-Sands had their excursion services, although Grange was hampered by the shoals of the Kent estuary. The most successful of all excursion steamers were those on the Lakes, established on Windermere just before the railways reached the lake, but much added to when the lines came to Windermere and Lakeside. Coniston and Ullswater also had their steamers, the former running in conjunction with the

Windermere vessels, both owned by the Furness Railway, to provide circular lakes tours using trains and horse drawn road coaches, the latter between Ambleside and Coniston.

Cargo services were less readily transferable to steam power because of the fuel problem. Only with the introduction of the economical compound engine in the mid nineteenth century was the steam coaster really possible, and the peak of operation was not reached until the 1890s and 1900s, by which time the triple expansion engine offered still further savings. Steam coasters came and went from all the north-west ports carrying every imaginable cargo, although minerals predominated, coal from Whitehaven and Maryport, iron ore to Workington, pig iron from Millom and Ulverston, grain to Silloth. Some of the ports handled larger, deep sea, steamships, notably Barrow-in-Furness, which was expected to be a second Liverpool. Unfortunately these hopes were not realized but there was a considerable traffic in iron ore until the ironworks at Hindpool closed in 1962. To-day bulk carriers come to Whitehaven with phosphate rock from Morocco for the Marchon chemical works but they cannot enter the port. Instead the cargo is transferred at sea to a large motor barge, the 'Odin'.

Along with their fast passenger ships the railway companies ran regular cargo sailings between North-west ports and Ireland, cattle being an important trade, and associated with their schedules were those operated by established short sea liner companies like Burns Laird. In more recent years there have been container services, from Heysham and Fleetwood, started by the London, Midland & Scottish Railway and superseded by the P. & O. . . roll on, roll-off. . . ferries between Fleetwood and Larne, an extension of the container principle.

Like everywhere else the north-west ports were well served by tugs and dredgers. In the days of sail tugs were vital to handle the ships, many of the larger ones had to be towed well clear of the port before they made sail, and a tug was particularly valuable in the tricky waters of the Duddon estuary. Indeed tugs were an early application of steam power, their value was at once apparent to sailing ship operators and in the north west they were stationed at Maryport as early as the 1850s. Nowadays there are none between the Solway and the Ribble, they come up from Liverpool when needed for launches at Barrow. This is because modern ships are more manoeuvrable, with their bridge controlled engines and bow thrust propellers.

Dredgers however remain, since all ports are plagued with siltation problems, caused by tidal behaviour, the sediment carried down by fresh water rivers, the spillage of cargo at the quays. With ships becoming larger and deeper, adequate dredging has become ever more pressing, not only to clear the port approaches but at the berths themselves, with oil terminals, usually some way offshore, as an additional problem. Port approaches can be kept clear by rapid action suction dredgers, but for accurate digging alongside quay walls the grab is needed. Nowadays much dredging work is put out to contract, more economical than the retention of a fleet of one's own.

Steam power revolutionized the fishing industry, by making distant water fishing possible. Sailing smacks were limited in range because they had to return to port before their catch became rotten. A steamer could go further, fish faster and return with her catch still in marketable condition. Hull, Grimsby and Aberdeen became the great East Coast distant water ports, Fleetwood the West Coast one, all with rail connections which allowed widespread distribution of the fish. The trawler became the most efficient fishing vessel, the trawl held open by otter boards which enabled a much wider net to be used than was possible with the beam trawl employed by the sailing smacks. As they became bigger, steam trawlers were able to fish further afield, from the Faroes to the White Sea, to Iceland, Spitzbergen and Bear Island. For many decades trawler design remained static, the classic 'sidewinder' with her gallows fore and aft, fish pounds on the fore deck and heavy winch forward of the wheelhouse. In the late 1940s diesel started to replace steam, but the real trawler revolution did not come until the 1960s with the arrival of the stern trawler after an extensive trials period. This has proved, with the addition of such refinements as net reels, gutting machines, freezing equipment and sonar detectors, so efficient that traditional grounds have been dangerously overfished. Fleetwood, as a distant water port, has suffered grieviously from the current recession, although a fair sized fleet of near water vessels survive, many of them miniature stern trawlers.

Morecambe Bay shrimps are nationally appreciated and these are caught with the beam trawl, nowadays towed by diesel powered vessels, which took over directly from sail.

In the days of sail and wood, shipyards were established up every creek and inlet where a good level site offered space to lay a keel. Iron and steam demanded far higher capital investment and shipbuilding became concentrated into industrial centres with ready access to ironworks and forges. In the north west new yards to build steamships were set up at Maryport, Workington, Whitehaven and Barrow-in-Furness, also later at Lytham, the Lytham yard having moved from Preston. Lytham was selected because it offered better launching facilities and the yard became specialists in the construction of stern wheel river steamers for the colonies. Barrow emerged as the greatest shipbuilding centre because the wide range of the tide allowed the largest vessels to be built. The yard concentrated on warships and under Vickers ownership from 1896, was able to build a battleship complete, armour, guns, turrets, engines and boilers. All could be made at Barrow. Submarine construction started in the very early days and the yard has remained the centre of British submarine design and building into the nuclear age.

Other north-west yards have long closed, mainly because of the depression between the wars, which brought great distress to West Cumberland. For example at Maryport, closure of Ritson's yard in 1914 and other later economic troubles, found 80 per cent of the town out of work. These yards had built many iron and steel sailing ships and only turned over to steam when sail had become uncompetitive, so they were not so deeply entrenched in steamship building as the Clyde and Tyne yards.

At the other end of a ship's life lies the breaker's yard and Barrow became a centre for this industry too, as did Preston and surprisingly Morecambe. Thomas W. Ward have closed their Barrow wharf but retain their business at Preston.

So within the limits of the Solway and the Ribble there has been a great variety of steamship activity. The following pages aim to portray this; the railway operated mail packets; the coasters, many of them locally owned at Barrow, Preston, Whitehaven; deep sea cargo steamers, tugs and dredgers, steam trawlers out of Fleetwood, the elegant white hulled excursion steamers of the Lakes, always called yachts, and finally the yards which built ships. A race apart from the commercial vessels were the steam yachts, mostly used on the Lakes, and particularly on Windermere. Few steam yachts were to be seen in Morecambe Bay, except for Sir James Ramsden's *Aries,* but on Windermere and Ullswater it was far otherwise, with craft ranging from 15 foot steam launches to Colonel Ridehalgh's *Britannia* later acquired by the Furness Railway as a floating directors' saloon. To-day the Windermere Steamboat Museum has preserved a remarkable collection of these crafts, now possibly the biggest concentration of steam vessels in the United Kingdom.

Edward Paget-Tomlinson, 1980.

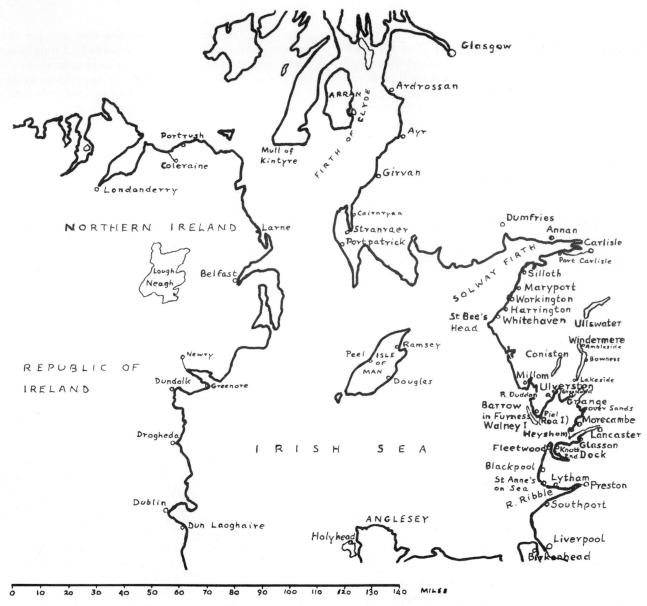

The Irish Sea, to illustrate the operation of steamship services between North West England, Scotland, the Isle of Man and Ireland.

Mail and Passenger Ships

Last of the Fleetwood-Belfast mail steamers were the turbine driven pair, the DUKE OF CUMBERLAND and the DUKE OF ARGYLL, completed by Denney's of Dumbarton in 1909.

At the zenith of cross channel passenger steamer operation in the north west before 1914, competion between owners was intense, each running their ships from their own port, the ports themselves frequently being creations of the shipowners if they were also railway companies, wealthy enough to undertake such capital expenditure to enlarge their influence. For the railways regarded their ships as extensions of their trains. Ireland was the chief target and at the height of their power the railways were using north-west ports from Silloth on the Solway to Fleetwood in the Fylde.

After the First World War economic problems caused considerable pruning of the cross channel services, over and above the disappearance of most of the competition due to the grouping of the railways in 1923. In the north west all the old companies came into the London, Midland & Scottish group with the exception of the North British at Silloth, part of the London & North Eastern. Nationalization of the railways in 1948 brought nationalization of their shipping services to the extinction of some and the improvement of others.

Steam packets have altered much in appearance. They could be described as conventional for many decades, although paddles gave way to screw and wood to iron. Naturally they became larger and faster, steam turbines replacing reciprocating engines and diesels triumphing over both. More recently convention has been thrown out to satisfy the demands of motor transport. The car ferry, or roll-on, roll-off ferry as it is now generally called, has undergone many variations in design to cater for larger vehicles, lorries rather than cars, and quicker turn round at the ports. They have been side loading, bow loading and stern loading, the last the more generally favoured.

Silloth

Silloth was a creation of the North British Railway who acquired the Port Carlisle Railway in 1862. This line replaced the old Carlisle Canal and was extended to Silloth in 1856 when a dock was built. Port Carlisle had had steamer services since 1826 but by the 1860s was badly silted, so Silloth became the new terminal for sailings to Liverpool, Dumfries, Douglas and Dublin. The Silloth Bay Steam Navigation Co. Ltd., was taken over by the North British Railway and new ships were built. Trade was not as good as was hoped, but continued with ships provided by R. Henderson & Son of Belfast until 1891. Thereafter William Sloan & Co., of Glasgow maintained the service with their purpose built 'Yarrow', in 1929 renamed 'Assaroe' when she passed to Palgrave Murphy of Dublin. The passenger services did not survive the Second World War.

Barrow-in-Furness

As a passenger port Barrow dates back to the opening of the Furness Railway down to Piel Pier (Roa Island) in 1846. Steamers were put on to Fleetwood and soon afterwards to Liverpool (a service from Ulverston to Liverpool had started in 1835). Early schedules seem to have been rather erratic (the tide would be one problem), but once the Furness Railway was extended to Carnforth with links to the London & North Western and the Midland, Barrow became a port of departure for Ireland and the Isle of Man for the Midland steamers which had been using Morecambe. A new company, the Barrow Steam Navigation Co. was formed in 1867 with Midland and Furness Railway support, allied with James Little & Co. of Glasgow, to run a service between Barrow and Belfast, using Piel Pier with a parallel service between Piel and Douglas. From 1881 the Barrow terminal was changed to Ramsden Dock. When Heysham was opened in 1904 the 'Barrow Route' declined and in 1907 the Barrow S.N. ships entered the Midland fleet.

Apart from the Furness Railway's participation in the Barrow S.N. ships, they did have a fleet of their own. In 1900 they revived the Fleetwood–Barrow excursion sailings, ordering a new paddle steamer, followed by three second hand ones. They also owned tugs, some of which were used for excursion traffic, plus a fleet of steamers on Windermere and Coniston described elsewhere.

Heysham

The Midland Railway came to the Irish Sea trade in 1851 with sailings between Morecambe and Belfast. These did not prove too satisfactory because of the difficult rail access to Morecambe. Then from 1867 Barrow became the terminal, but rail links were still difficult. The solution was a new port which could be entered at any state of the tide. Heysham near Morecambe was chosen and opened in 1904, with all the year round sailings to Belfast and summer sailings to Douglas. Four passenger ships were ordered, each from a different builder, two with triple expansion engines and two with turbines. Two were sold to the Isle of Man Steam Packet Co., one of which, the *Manxman* remained afloat until after the Second World War, one was a war loss in 1917 and one passed to the new Tilbury–Dunkirk service in 1927.

By this time the London, Midland & Scottish Railway was in command at Heysham and Fleetwood and three new ships were completed in 1928 to replace both the Midland vessels and the Fleetwood ones, all sailings now being concentrated at Heysham. They took the Duke names associated with Fleetwood, the new Dukes being larger ships with long careers ahead of them. They were joined by a fourth 'Duke' in 1935 although she went to the East Coast in 1949. The first three Dukes lasted until 1956 when they were replaced by three new ships of the same name. These remained in service until closure of the Heysham–Belfast service in 1975, although one, the *Duke of Rothesay* had been converted into a car ferry for the Fishguard–Rosslare service in 1967. More recently Heysham has become the terminal for the Manx Line's roll-on roll-off ferry service to Douglas, while Fishers of Barrow operate container ship sailings to Belfast and Douglas with a considerable terminal at Heysham.

Fleetwood

Fleetwood was nothing at all until Peter Hesketh of Rossall Hall built a town, to which in 1840 he brought the railway from Preston. The railway encouraged a port to develop and a steam packet service to Ulster was soon established, actually in 1843, by the North Lancashire Steam Navigation Company, a subsidiary of F. Kemp & Co. of Fleetwood. Kemp's ran packets from Fleetwood to Ardrossan, and Glasgow to Londonderry as well as from Fleetwood to Belfast and Londonderry, with a mail contract from 1850. The Fleetwood–Irish services to Belfast and Londonderry passed in 1870 to the joint management of the London

& North Western and the Lancashire & Yorkshire Railways who soon replaced an ageing fleet of paddle steamers by some new ones, three of which were built at Barrow, the first of these being the *Duke of Connaught* of 1875. The Duke names became associated with Fleetwood's nightly Irish services and some very fine ships were added to the fleet. The *Duke of Clarence* of 1892 built by Laird's passed in 1906 to the Lancashire & Yorkshire Railway who put her on a new service from Hull to Zeebrugge. More Dukes followed from Denny's, Vickers' and John Brown's, the final pair being turbine driven with three screws and two funnels.

In 1928 the London, Midland & Scottish Railway ended the Fleetwood sailings and concentrated everything at Heysham. Only recently has Fleetwood come to the fore again as a passenger port with the establishment in 1975 of the P. & O's roll-on, roll-off ferry to Larne and Dublin. The two ships the *Bison* and the *Buffalo*, assisted by another ship on the Larne run, sail daily on each service, unit load trailers being the principal traffic. Passenger accommodation is limited.

Paddle box of the Furness Railway's paddle steamer LADY EVELYN built in 1900 for the Fleetwood-Barrow service.

Top left: S.S. *Assaroe* berthing at Silloth. She was built in 1893 as the *Yarrow* for William Sloan of Glasgow, who had become involved in the Silloth–Dublin sailings. In 1929 a new company was formed, the Dublin & Silloth Steamship Co. Ltd., under the managership of Palgrave Murphy of Dublin. The *Yarrow* was taken over and renamed *Assaroe* with a buff, black topped funnel, and a green band under the black. Passengers, cargo and cattle continued to be carried until 1939 when the service was suspended. The *Assaroe* herself went on to other duties and was scrapped in 1947. (*Malcolm Wilson.*)

Bottom left: for a while in 1912–13 the Isle of Man Steam Packet Company ran steamer sailings to Douglas from Whitehaven. The screw mail steamer *Tynwald* was built on the Clyde in 1891 and lasted until 1930 with the Isle of Man Steam Packet Co. Later she became a steam yacht. Also engaged in this service was the paddle steamer *Mona's Queen* built at Barrow in 1885. (*Whitehaven Museum.*) See Cover Picture.

Paddle steamer *Manxman* of the Barrow Steam Navigation Co.,
leaving Maryport. She was built in 1870 as the *Antrim* for the
company's Belfast service but was re-named on her transfer to the
Douglas route. She was withdrawn and scrapped in 1902. (*Miss Annie
Robinson, Maryport Maritime Museum.*)

Top left: Built for the Barrow Steam Navigation Company's services to Douglas and Belfast, the *Duchess of Devonshire* was launched by Vickers in 1897. When Barrow was given up after 1907 the ship moved to Heysham and was eventually sold in 1928 for further service out of Gibraltar. A 1905 scene leaving Barrow. (*Jonathan Wignall.*)

Bottom left: To bring Blackpool tourists direct to Barrow and put them onto Furness Railway metals to visit the Lakes, the company acquired a fleet of paddle steamers, the first being ordered in 1900 from Scott's of Kinghorn on the Forth. She was the *Lady Evelyn*, remaining with the company until 1914, later passing to the South Coast's Campbell fleet as the *Brighton Belle*. Another ship, the *Lady Moyra*, was acquired in 1910. Like the *Evelyn* she passed to the Campbell fleet after the 1914–18 War and again like the *Lady Evelyn* was lost at Dunkirk. (*Raymond Sankey.*)

Compound paddle engines of the Furness Railway's *Lady Evelyn*, built in 1900. The engine room staff pose proudly behind their gleaming charge, the view being taken from the control platform. (*Raymond Sankey.*)

Top left: Built for the new Heysham–Belfast and Douglas services in 1904, the triple expansion engined *Antrim*, the first of the four ships ordered. She came from John Brown's yard at Clydebank and remained on the Heysham–Belfast service until 1928. Then the Isle of Man Steam Packet Company bought her for their Heysham–Douglas service, renaming her *Ramsey Town*. She was scrapped in 1936. (*Raymond Sankey.*)

Bottom left: Fourth of the Midland quartet was the turbine *Manxman* built by Vickers at Barrow in 1904. She passed to the Isle of Man Steam Packet Company in 1920 without change of name and was withdrawn in 1949. (*Raymond Sankey.*)

Top right: To replace the railway operated steamers on the Fleetwood and Heysham to Belfast services the London, Midland & Scottish Railway commissioned three new ships from Denny's of Dumbarton in 1928, followed by a fourth from Harland & Wolff in 1935. they all used Heysham as their base, but took the Duke names associated with Fleetwood. This is the *Duke of Argyll* which with her two sisters lasted until 1956.

Bottom right: Coming alongside at Heysham, the turbine *Duke of Lancaster*, the first of three new passenger and mail steamers built in 1955/6 to replace the old Dukes. The *Duke of Lancaster* remained on the Heysham service until it closed in 1976, by that time adapted to load cars through stern doors. Earlier in her career she had done summer cruises to the West Highlands, Scandinavia and Holland. (*Author.*)

Left: Built by Vickers for the night service between Fleetwood and Belfast and Londonderry the *Duke of Cornwall* was completed in 1898, a handsome vessel. She flies the house flag of her first owners, the London & North Western and Lancashire & Yorkshire Railways. This ship had a long career, passing to the Isle of Man Steam Packet Company in 1928 who kept her, as the *Rushen Castle*, on their Douglas–Heysham service. She was broken up in 1947. (*Vickers Shipbuilding Group Ltd.*)

Excursion Steamers

Over and above the regular passenger and mail services there were numerous excursion sailings from north-west ports. These were usually summer only, the major operator being the Isle of Man Steam Packet Co. Their Fleetwood–Douglas service was started in the nineteenth century as early as 1842 and lasted until 1961 but has since been revived.

Many vessels worked on shorter excursion services in Morecambe Bay; Morecambe to Blackpool, Barrow to Morecambe, even Morecambe to Grange-over-Sands. Some of these were tugs with a passenger certificate, such as the Midland Railway's 'Wyvern' based on Heysham, others were purpose built pleasure steamers such as the *Robina* owned by the New Morecambe Central Pier Co. Ltd.

Below: Isle of Man Steam Packet Company's *Viking*, her last sailing before withdrawal, to Douglas from Fleetwood, in 1954. She had been built at Newcastle in 1905. (*Blackpool Gazette and Herald.*)

Left: Last sailing of the *Mona's Isle* from Fleetwood to Douglas in September 1961. This had been a regular summer excursion for over a hundred years. Fortunately after pier improvements at Fleetwood it has been revived and has proved as popular as ever. (*Blackpool Gazette and Herald.*)

Above: The screw steamer *Robina* was a small excursion vessel run by the New Morecambe Central Pier Co. Ltd., operating between Central Pier and Blackpool, Fleetwood and Barrow in the years before 1914. (*Keith Willacy collection, Merseyside County Museums.*)

Left: Sailing between North Pier, Blackpool, St. Anne's and Southport, the paddle steamer *Bickerstaffe* was built in 1879 at Birkenhead for the Blackpool Passenger Steamboat Co. Ltd. (*John Clarkson.*)

Below: The Morecambe Bay excursion paddler *Roses* built in 1876 for the Morecambe Steam Boat Co. Ltd. (*Alan Lockett collection.*)

Cargo steamers

A frequent visitor to Whitehaven in the 1930's, the Newry Steam coaster OPEPE, owned by Joseph Fisher & Sons Ltd., of Newry, who named their ships after trees. From a photograph at Whitehaven Museum.

Because of the heavy coal consumption of the early steamships they were uneconomic as cargo carriers, the coal took up too much space. This was particularly the case with deep sea cargo ships when overseas coaling stations were widely spaced. Short range coasters did not suffer so much, but sail, because of its cheapness, remained dominant in the coastal trade throughout the nineteenth century.

Between the Solway and the Ribble most of the cargoes were local, either coastal or to and from Ireland. Only Barrow had an extensive dock system designed for large steamships, Barrow having great hopes of rivalling Liverpool. Ocean going steamers did come into Maryport, Workington and Whitehaven, also Fleetwood and Preston, but most of the local ports depended on the nearby trades, coal to Ireland, pig iron coastwise, Irish cattle, European grain, Spanish

ore. There were several local coastal steamship owners; Fisher's of Barrow who moved from sail to steam, Kennaugh's of Whitehaven, Williamson's of Workington and Gardner's of Lancaster. Hine Brothers of Maryport used to own sailing ships in the Australian trade, but their steamers were mostly limited to home waters or the Continental trades.

To carry as much cargo as possible, coastal steamers early adopted the screw propeller, siting the engines aft to give the maximum of cargo space. To increase hold capacity and to accommodate larger engines and boilers the raised quarterdeck design became widely adopted from the late 1870s. This was the time when the old simple expansion engine was being replaced by the economical compound, followed by the even more economical triple expansion.

West Cumberland

During the nineteenth century Silloth, Maryport, Workington and Whitehaven handled considerable cargoes. At Silloth, founded in 1856, Carr's established their flour mills in the 1880s and a cattle lairage was built. Both grain and cattle are dominant trades today, with a new lairage.

Maryport as a port dated from the mid eighteenth century and a tidal dock was built in 1836, enlarged and deepened two years later. With the opening of the Maryport & Carlisle Railway in 1845 far more traffic came in and two enclosed docks were opened, the Elizabeth in 1857, the Senhouse in 1884. Coal was the main export, plus steel rails rolled at Workington, Maryport importing iron ore for the Workington blast furnaces.

For Workington's Lonsdale dock, opened in 1865, was too small for the greater tonnage of deep sea steamers. Eventually in 1927 the larger Prince of Wales dock was opened and Maryport trade suffered. This dock, originally owned by the steelworks, but now under the control of the District Council, handles iron ore imports and the export trade of steel rails, whose production is now concentrated at Workington.

Whitehaven was in the eighteenth century the third port of Britain, because of her considerable tobacco and sugar imports and coal and iron exports. The tidal harbour was extended by dock and pier construction in the nineteenth century. The piers increased the area of sheltered water and the dock, Queen's, opened in 1876, gave more berths. Other Whitehaven traffics were iron and iron products from Workington. Both Workington and Whitehaven had their fleets of steam coasters. R. Williamson & Son of Workington were shipbuilders who from the 1890s built coasters for their own fleet which eventually in 1938 passed into the management of Joseph Constantine of Middlesbrough. W. S. Kennaugh of Whitehaven started in steam in 1883 with the *Scale Force* and built up a fleet of ever larger coasters, all named after Lake District waterfalls. In 1908 they moved to Liverpool but their ships were always registered at Whitehaven.

Nowadays Whitehaven is busy with open cast coal exports and the import of phosphate rock from Casablanca for the Marchon Chemical Works above the town.

Millom, Barrow-in-Furness, Ulverston

Millom, or Borwick Rails consisted of two open tidal quays built for the ironworks traffic, pig iron and Hodbarrow haematite ore being the main exports. Most of this was handled by topsail schooners during the nineteenth century and indeed up to 1914, but Hay's and Robertson's of Glasgow and Savage's of Liverpool all operated steamers into the Duddon.

Barrow-in-Furness had great ambitions as an international port, to export the products of the iron and steel works founded in the late 1850s. Sir James Ramsden was the main driving force behind the massive dock construction which followed, the Furness Railway raising the funds, to which the Duke of Devonshire contributed handsomely. The Act for the new port was passed in 1863 and the first dock, the Devonshire was opened in 1867, the year Barrow became a borough. The Buccleuch followed in 1869 and the Ramsden in 1879, but the final one, the Cavendish, was never completed. These docks did not fill with the large vessels the promoters expected, save for the Anchor Line ships which used Ramsden Dock. Grain, jute and pulp were principal imports for Barrow industries, and Spanish ore came in for the ironworks, to supplement and eventually replace the local haematite.

Barrow commercial interests never succeeded in founding their own line of deep sea ships although they tried in the 1870s to start a fleet of steamers to import Calcutta jute. But the old established coasting firm of James Fisher & Sons have had an enterprising history. They started in sail in 1847 and built up a big fleet. Their first steamer was commissioned in 1883 and their first motor vessel in 1931. They have participated in the container traffic between Heysham, Fleetwood and Belfast and in 1966 built two roll-on roll-off ferries for delivering heavy machinery to coastal power stations; in earlier days their ships had been given specially wide and long hatches to load gun turrets for warships building at Barrow. A recent involvement has been the operation of nuclear fuel carriers.

Ulverston became a port when the canal opened in 1796, but steamers rarely used it, save at the very end of its career, when Joseph Monks & Co. Ltd., Liverpool, coasters came with provisions for Ulverston shops and hides and extract for the tannery. The last traffic came to the canal in 1917, but the North Lonsdale Iron & Steel Co. had their own pier for the shipment of pig iron. Fisher's and Savage's ships were frequent callers at Ainslie Pier, but in 1939 the furnaces closed down and the pier fell into disuse.

Heysham and Glasson Dock

Apart from the passenger sailings the Midland Railway developed Heysham as a cargo port, in particular for the Irish cattle trade. G. & J. Burns (later Burns Laird) ships ran a regular schedule to Londonderry. In 1936 the London, Midland & Scottish Railway added a turbine steamer the *Slieve Bearnagh* which remained on the Heysham–Belfast run until withdrawal in 1971. In 1958 two container ships were placed on this route, both now withdrawn, but a cargo service is operated by Fisher's of Barrow, importing fruit, while both Sealink, the maritime division of the British Railways Board and Fisher's operate container sailings, the latter with large terminal facilities at Heysham.

Glasson Dock at the mouth of the Lune was opened in 1787 by the Lancaster Port Commissioners as a more satisfactory harbour than Lancaster itself and was added to in 1825 when the Lancaster Canal's branch reached it. The dock became busy with coastal shipping, mostly sail, although it was seriously affected by the opening of Preston Dock in 1892. A branch railway from Lancaster, opened in 1883, helped and the dock was used by the Lancaster steam coaster owner Robert Gardner. There was a revival of traffic from 1969 with a container service to the Isle of Man and Northern Ireland, but this finished in 1976. Today grain comes in, also sea dredged aggregate and scrap metal.

Fleetwood

The smart passenger steamers which operated the nightly Belfast and Londonderry services also carried cargo, but the railway companies ran no purely cargo ships from here. In 1928 the Fleetwood sailings were discontinued, but in the 1950s a container service was put on to Belfast and via Belfast to Stranraer. These were not the large modern containers, but the handy sized ones used by the London, Midland & Scottish Railway from the 1930s. Fishers of Barrow provided the ships. It was replaced by the P. & O. Line's roll-on roll-off ferry, started in 1975 with two large ships, the *Bison* and the *Buffalo,* assisted by a third. They run to Larne and Dublin and can carry no less than 130 trailer units. The tractors do not normally travel with their trailers but take over at each terminal.

Preston

The Ribble was in use for commercial navigation in the Middle Ages, but not until the seventeenth century could Preston properly be called a port, limited to the coastal and Irish trades. The opening of the Douglas Navigation by 1742 helped Preston industry, since coal could now come from Wigan by water, but improvements to the Ribble itself were delayed until the nineteenth century, started under an Act of 1806. Further river improvements were undertaken in the 1840s, which included training walls. By this time trade was increasing, a dock was built at Lytham in 1842 and new quays were built by Preston Corporation in 1844. In the end the Ribble became so busy that an enclosed dock was found necessary, for which an Act was passed in 1883, the former Ribble Navigation Company, the third of such ventures, being acquired by Preston Corporation. In 1892 the dock, no less than 3,200 feet long, was opened, but more river improvements were needed, added depth being achieved by further training walls to speed the scour of the ebb tide. Imports grew in the years between the wars, with coal to Ireland as a principal export. From 1948 to 1974 Preston was the terminal of a new venture, the Atlantic Steam Navigation Co. Ltd., who started a roll-on roll-off ferry service to Larne, mainly for lorries. Following chartered tonnage, two new ships were ordered in 1957–8, the *Bardic Ferry* and *Ionic Ferry*. In recent years ferry services from Fleetwood have competed very seriously with Preston.

James Fisher of Barrow ran their steam coaster FORD FISHER to the North Lonsdale ironworks pier below Canal Foot, Ulverston. She had been built on the Severn at Sudbrook in 1913 but did not come to Fisher's until after the 1914-18 War. Her shallow draught allowed her easier access to the pier than the more conventional coaster. From a photograph in the possession of John Wilson, Ulverston.

Left: Silloth in the 1920s with (top) a steam coaster of the Liverpool fleet of J. S. Monks Ltd., alongside Carr's flour mills, who continue to take considerable tonnages of seaborne grain; and (bottom) a ship of the Zillah fleet loading coal. (*Malcolm Wilson.*)

Maryport as a 'port', with the crowded Senhouse dock. An 1890s
view. (*Miss Annie Robinson, Maryport Maritime Museum.*)

Top left: Aground off Maryport, Richard Hughes' *Wild Rose*, one of his 'Rose' fleet of coasters. Her home port was Liverpool, but Hughes' ships were mainly crewed from Anglesey, hence their nickname the 'Welsh Navy'. (*Miss Annie Robinson, Maryport Maritime Museum.*)

Bottom left: The Lonsdale dock, Workington in 1907, busy with steam coasters. (*Cumbria County Libraries, Workington.*)

Left: Queen's Dock, Whitehaven in 1895. The *Sapphire*, one of Robertson's 'Gem' Line of Glasgow, loading stone by chute from side tipping railway wagons. She was built in 1881. The dock shunting locomotive is of especial interest. (*Whitehaven Museum.*)

Right: S.S. *Colwith Force*, built in 1918 by R. Williamson & Son of Workington for W. S. Kennaugh & Co. of Liverpool, but originating from Whitehaven where the ships were registered. She is a characteristic raised quarterdeck ship with two long hatches. (*John Clarkson.*)

The Whitehaven coaster *Cumbria* built in 1914. At the time of this photograph, about 1950, she was managed by T. W. Dixon of Whitehaven. (*Whitehaven Museum.*)

Larne built in 1922, the raised quarterdeck coaster *Stainburn* owned
by Henry Reynolds of Whitehaven. She was mainly in the coal trade
to the Isle of Man and Ireland. (*Whitehaven Museum.*)

Left: At the Walney Island sand wharf in 1948 the steam coaster *Ophir* loading gravel. She was owned by Savage's of Liverpool. The wharf remained in use until 1964 served by steam cranes and narrow gauge vertical boilered steam locomotives. It was operated by various firms, including for a time Coast Lines. (*Jonathan Wignall collection; photo North-Western Evening Mail, Barrow.*)

Top left: Millom ironworks quay in about 1930, with the Glasgow coaster *The Duke* waiting to load pig iron. *The Duke* built in 1927, 820 gross tons, was owned by John Hay of Glasgow. John Hay's ships were frequent callers at the Duddon port. (*Jonathan Wignall collection, photographed by Mr Lamb of Millom.*)

Bottom left: Ramsden Dock, Barrow in the 1930s with hydraulic cranes unloading iron ore into hopper wagons from the Swedish steamer *Torne*. She was one of the fleet of the Grangesberg–Oxelösund iron mining concern. (*Furness Museum.*)

Barrow Docks handled large tonnages of iron ore for the Hindpool works. In 1956 the Swedish steamer *Saltarö* is unloading. She went aground off Barrow the following year and was broken up by Ward's. (*Author.*)

Above: Ainslie Pier, Ulverston, was built by the North Lonsdale Iron & Steel Co. Ltd. in 1874 to ship pig iron. They had two small steamers of their own but relied on coaster firms like Fisher's of Barrow and Savage's of Liverpool. After some years of closure due to slack trade, the pier was re-opened in 1932. The first vessel to berth was the motor coaster *Warita* owned by John Summers' steelworks at Shotton, Flint. She loaded a cargo of pig iron for the Deeside works. (*Alan Lawson.*)

Right: Fisher's steam coaster *Lough Fisher* built in 1921, a motor vessel of the same name was completed in 1950. (*John Clarkson.*)

Above: Disaster in the Manchester Ship Canal to the Ulverston owned *City of Liverpool.* This was one of two ships owned by the North Lonsdale Iron & Steel Co., an ex-Weaver salt packet 88 ft. long built in 1885 at Winsford. North Lonsdale had her from 1889 to 1916. On this occasion she capsized in the Ship Canal because her cargo of pig iron had shifted. When it was lifted out, she righted herself. (*John Wilson.*)

Right and top right: Well and truly aground on Foulney Island near Barrow, the Newry steam coaster *Oak* owned by Joseph Fisher's Newry and Kilkeel Steamship Co. Ltd. and built in 1906. In a similar predicament is the North Lonsdale Iron & Steel Co's *City of Liverpool,* the ex-Weaver salt packet, very small for sea trading. Both ships are unloading ballast, so that they have some chance of floating off at the next high water. And underneath, awaiting a buyer, the North Lonsdale Iron & Steel Company's *City of Liverpool* tied up in the Ulverston Canal. She was eventually sold in 1916 to a Liverpool lighterage firm. (*Robert Inman.*)

Heysham once handled iron ore, a scene at the wharf in about 1910. The steamer is Spanish, registered at Bilbao. Carnforth ironworks would take much of the ore. (*Keith Willacy.*)

Top left: To handle the cargo and cattle traffic between Belfast and Heysham hitherto dealt with by the passenger ships, the London, Midland & Scottish Railway built an extra ship, the turbine *Slieve Bearnagh*, completed by Denny's of Dumbarton in 1936. She followed the design of the Holyhead cargo and cattle vessels and the same style of naming. Her cattle were driven off and on through side doors and her electric cranes were designed for rapid cargo work. The mainmast was later resited as here to allow more space for containers aft. (*Author.*)

Bottom left: Fleetwood was the home of a large chemical works opened in 1900 by the United Alkali Co. Ltd., who were merged into the I.C.I. giant in 1926. They had their own ships, carrying limestone from North Wales to Fleetwood, named after chemical elements. A view of the *Sodium* in United Alkali colours. She was built in 1923. (*John Clarkson.*)

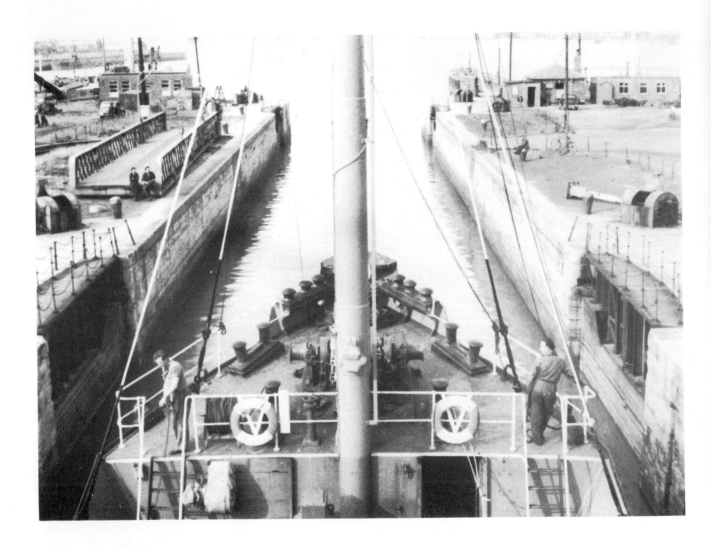

During the 1950's Fisher's of Barrow ran a container service between
Fleetwood, Belfast and Stranraer. Their ships were chartered by
British Railways. The containers were of the small kind introduced
during the 1930s, the ships not being specially designed. This is the
Lough Fisher leaving Wyre Dock, Fleetwood. She was built in 1950.
(*Author.*)

The modern roll-on roll-off ferry berth at Fleetwood used by the P & O's Larne and Dublin ferries. The *Buffalo*, a big ship of 3484 gross tons was built in 1975. (*Author.*)

Top left: An impressive ship, the *Ionic Ferry* was built by Denny of Dumbarton in 1958 for the Preston-Larne ferry service of the Atlantic Steam Navigation Co. Ltd., founded in 1948 and initially using chartered tonnage. A sister, the *Bardic Ferry*, had been built in 1957 also for the Preston run, the first ship the company actually owned. In 1974 the Preston–Larne service was ended but the *Ionic Ferry* had already gone to start a new service to Larne from Cairnryan. Eventually in 1976 she was sold to Italy. She loaded vehicles through stern doors and had two car and lorry decks, plus passenger accommodation. (*John Clarkson.*)

Bottom left: Well known at Preston until the 1960s were Hugh Craig and Company's coasters. The company, founded in Belfast in 1842, were coal importers, operating sailing ships. This vessel, the *Helen Craig*, built in 1891, was their first steamer. She lasted until 1959, latterly operating entirely between Belfast and Preston where she became so famous that her final departure was marked by a civic ceremony. In her early days, fitted with a towing hook, she had acted as a tug for Craig's schooners. (*John Clarkson.*)

Tugs

Millom harbour tug HARDBACK owned by the Hodbarrow Mining Company and built in 1901 helping a steam coaster out of the Duddon port. Sketched from an old postcard.

In the days of sail, tugs were vital to handle sailing ships in and out of port. Indeed towing was an early application of steam power; the value of independence from wind and tide could be instantly appreciated by the sailing ship master and tugs were among the pioneer steamship designs. One only has to think of the tug *Charlotte Dundas* on the Forth & Clyde Canal, among Britain's first successful steamboats, built in 1802. Tugs did not have to worry about bunker space and excessive fuel consumption. Below decks they could be all engine, boilers and coal.

In the north west of England tugs were introduced at an early date, to Maryport in the 1850s, to Whitehaven a little later. They were paddle tugs, the paddles giving great manoeuvrability if one could be dis-

connected, and equal power ahead and astern. For towage, paddles remained in favour during the nineteenth century and beyond, but screw tugs were introduced in the 1880s. Barrow had her first tug, the paddler *Walney* in 1868;, her first screw tug was the *Furness* delivered in 1898. A second paddle *Walney* also carried passengers as did the screw tug *Devonshire*. At Barrow tugs had the extra duties of attending launches, handling completed ships and for that matter towing ships to Ward's breaking up berth.

At Heysham the Midland used their *Wyvern* for passenger excursions as well as towage, while Fleetwood had a tug, the *Adjutant* delivered new in 1858. Better known here was *Cleveleys* built in 1902 and replaced by a second *Cleveleys* in 1929.

Paddle tug *Florence* built in 1879 by R. Williamson at Harrington, the last vessel to be completed at this yard, for service at Maryport. In this picture she has two towropes out, forming a bridle, presumably linked to a sailing ship. *(Whitehaven Museum.)*

A common sight at Maryport in the 1900s, two tugs berthing a four masted barque, the stern of the second tug can only just be seen, obscured by the tow. *(Miss Annie Robinson, Maryport Maritime Museum.)*

Owned by John Collins of Whitehaven the harbour tug *Prince of Wales* alongside the Sugar Tongue at Whitehaven. This quay, reminiscent of the great West Indies trade which Whitehaven once enjoyed, is now a berth for fishing boats. The *Prince of Wales* was built in 1862 at Hull. *(Whitehaven Museum.)*

Top left: Launch of the battleship *Vanguard* at Barrow in February, 1909, the biggest ship Vickers had so far built. But this picture is chosen rather to illustrate the tug *Furness* built by J. P. Rennoldson of South Shields in 1898 for work at the port of Barrow, including attendance at launches. *(Vickers Shipbuilding Group Ltd.)*

Bottom left: Grossly overcrowded and an affront to the Board of Trade, the Barrow paddle tug *Walney* returning from a football match at Blackpool. Like the *Wyvern* the Furness Railway's *Walney* doubled as an excursion steamer when needed. Built in 1904 she lasted until 1951, latterly, from 1930, based at Troon. *(Raymond Sankey.)*

Entering Barrow Docks in July 1955, the cruiser *Australia* in the charge of the tug *Fishershill*, on her way to Ward's breaking up berth. The *Australia* was built in 1927, the tug *Fishershill* in 1946 as the *Empire Hilda,* one of the wartime design of general service tugs. James Fisher & Sons Ltd., of Barrow acquired her in 1949. *(K. E. Royall.)*

Top left: Preston tug *Energy* built at Preston in 1899 for service at the Port of Preston. Preston tugs and dredgers carry the town's coat of arms, the Paschal Lamb, on the funnel. *(John Clarkson.)*

Bottom left: Both tug and excursion steamer, the Midland Railway's *Wyvern* stationed at Heysham. She was built by Ferguson Brothers, Port Glasgow in 1905 and named after the mythical wyvern in the Midland Railway coat of arms. She lasted until 1960. *(John Clarkson.)*

Overleaf: The *Wyvern* as a tug in Midland colours, registered like all Heysham ships, at Lancaster. *(Keith Willacy collection, Merseyside County Museums.)*

Dredgers

Whitehaven's steam dredger CLEARWAY at work in the days when she had a steam grab crane. She was built at Aberdeen in 1927 and after a recent refit, now with a diesel crane, she looks good for many more years. Sketch based on a photograph by Larry Park of Whitehaven.

Harbour works demand constant maintenance, the biggest single item being dredging. Silt and spoil accumulate for a variety of reasons, deposited by the tide, carried down by fresh water rivers, eroded from banks; while during cargo working, it is inevitable that material is dropped overside. There are really two dredging problems, keeping the harbour approaches clear, and maintenance of adequate depth in the port itself. Often the harbour approaches can be cleared by so directing the flow of the tide that it keeps a channel scoured clear. Training walls and piers can achieve this, for example the Lune is channelled between stone embankments which speed up the tide, sweeping the silt held in suspension out to sea. Otherwise a dredger has to dig the silt out of the channel, by suction pump, a ladder of buckets or by grab. If there is any obstacle to the seaward progress of the silt it will form a mound or bar. This happens at the harbour mouth at Whitehaven where the two piers form a barrier, against which the ebb piles up stone, shingle and colliery waste which can form a bar 50 feet wide and 5 feet high. Buckets and grabs have been used to clear this obstruction, by digging a series of holes in a line across the harbour mouth, the ebb having to fill the holes before it can create a bar.

Buckets and grabs are the best means of dredging against quay walls, particularly grabs which can be dropped right up to the wall foot. Nowadays dredgers are either of the grab type or suction, with pumps powerful enough to lift sand and shingle.

Maryport dredger *Netherhall* at work by the entrance to the Senhouse Dock (off the picture to the right). She was built in 1897, and named after the Senhouse mansion at Maryport. *(Miss Annie Robinson, Maryport Maritime Museum.)*

Bucket dredger in Whitehaven harbour, photographed in 1904. She was a wooden hulled craft, not self propelled but manouevred by warps and windlasses. The ladder boom and frame were of wood. Note the bevel drive to the big wheel at the upper end of the chain of buckets, lifted clear in this picture. *(Whitehaven Museum.)*

Whitehaven's steam dredger *Clearway* built by Alexander Hall at Aberdeen in 1927. Now fitted with a diesel grab crane she works on the clearance of the bar at the port entrance, as well as within the harbour as in this view. After two and a half hours dredging her hoppers are full and she proceeds into the Bay to dump her spoil. *(Larry Park.)*

Top left: Dredging activity in Buccleuch Dock, Barrow-in-Furness; the presumably Furness Railway dredger No. 4, about which I can find no details, lifting spoil into F.R. self propelled hopper No. 3, built in 1907. The bucket ladder is well down, so she is dredging pretty deep. *(Raymond Sankey.)*

Bottom left: Working in the Walney Channel and at Heysham for many years, the bow well bucket dredger *Piel* was built by Ferguson Brothers of Port Glasgow in 1927 for the London, Midland & Scottish Railway. She was self propelled with her own spoil hopper, remaining in service until 1950. *(K. E. Royall.)*

Fitting out at the P. K. Harris shipyard at Appledore in October 1960, the *Red Nab*, a self propelled diesel hopper based on Heysham. She carries dredged spoil for dumping at sea. *(Author.)*

Trawlers

The TRENT, owned by the Wyre Steam Trawling Co. Ltd., of Fleetwood, was built in 1904 at North Shields. Note the fishing gallows fore and aft and the dan buoys lashed to the shrouds, used to mark the fishing grounds.

Fleetwood, the creation of the Hesketh family, became a fishing port in the 1840s, fishermen coming to the Wyre from the silted up creeks around Southport. Houses were built for them and they built up a flourishing shrimping industry, while their smacks, cutter and ketch rigged, trawled for bottom feeding fish in the Irish Sea and further afield. Some men from the pioneer trawling port of Brixham moved to Fleetwood, as they did to Hull and Grimsby, as a base for operations further afield.

The fishing industry was helped by the building of Wyre Dock, started in 1869 by the Lancashire and Yorkshire Railway and completed after serious financial setbacks in 1876. In 1906 part of Wyre Dock was converted into a fish dock for the steam trawlers which had now replaced the sailing smacks. Steam trawlers were introduced in the late 1870s. At first they were converted paddle tugs, but in 1881 Earle's yard at Hull launched the steam screw trawler *Zodiac* for Grimsby owners. She was really a sailing smack with a small steam engine, but trawler design evolved very quickly and by the 1900s some powerful vessels were being built, 120 feet in length, and capable of staying at sea for three weeks. These ships opened up the distant water fisheries of the White Sea, Bear Island and Spitzbergen.

Fleetwood's steam trawler industry became linked with the growing fleets of Hull and Grimsby, in particular the Marr and Boston interests. Fleetwood ranked third after the two Humber ports, but in common with them has suffered grievously by the limitations of the Icelandic fishery. The conventional side fishing trawler or 'sidewinder' is now almost extinct, the bulk of the work being done by the efficient and less harsh stern trawler, in which the fish can be gutted in sheltered conditions.

Left: Nowadays Wyre Dock, Fleet-wood does not present such a crowded scene. This must be Christmas with so many steam trawlers in port, not all based on Fleetwood. *(British Transport Docks Board, Fleetwood.)*

Right: Coaling a trawler at Fleet-wood in 1956. The twin spouts fill both wing bunkers simultaneously, avoiding trimming problems. Prominent in the foreground is a dan buoy used to mark fishing grounds. *(Author.)*

Left: Built in 1906 the *Gladys* FD 61 was owned by the Fleetwood Steam Fishing Co. Ltd. *(Raymond Sankey.)*

Right: A typical steam trawler of the 1920s–30s, the *Edward Walmsley* was owned by the Scarisbrick Steam Trawling Company. She was built at South Shields by J. P. Rennoldson in 1919. *(John Clarkson)*

Carrying drums of fish offal the steam lighter *Sea Maid* in Wyre Dock, Fleetwood in 1956. She was built by Dunston's at Thorne, Yorkshire in 1948. *(Author.)*

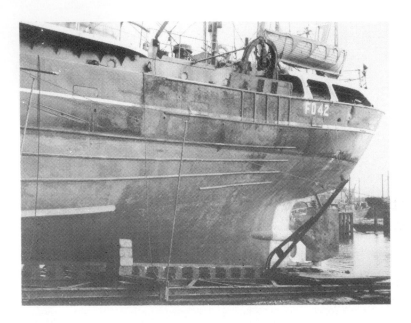

Top left: The *Boston Seafoam* FD 42 a motor trawler built in 1956, on the repair slip at Fleetwood, February 1960. The after gallows and trawl door are clearly seen. (*Author.*)

Diesel power slowly replaced reciprocating steam during the 1950s. The *Armana* was built in 1962 for J. Marr & Son Ltd., who have ships based on Hull and Fleetwood. Subsequently she was sold to Cape Town. (*John Clarkson.*)

Top left: With the introduction of the stern trawler the old shape changed radically. Marr's *Jacinta* built at Wallsend in 1972 has a gantry over the stern for handling the net which is drawn up a ramp. *(David Buckley.)*

Bottom left: Small stern trawler *Boston Blenheim* FD 137. She was built by Richard Dunston at Hessle on the Humber in 1972 for Boston Deep Sea Fisheries Ltd., to operate out of Fleetwood. Note the travelling block on the wire between mast and gantry, for lifting the cod end of the net in which the fish are trapped. When the cod end is opened the fish spill down a chute to the gutting deck below. *(John Clarkson.)*

First applied to distant water fishing the stern trawler concept has been introduced to the near water side of the industry in recent years, where prospects are brighter. A lot of small trawlers like these are based on Fleetwood, and work in the Irish Sea. The trawl with its doors is towed directly over the stern, while the gantry handles the net inboard, as in the distant water ships. *(Author.)*

Lakes Steamers

Arrival of the railway brought development to the Lake District, hotels, piers, boats for hire and steamers. When roads were narrow and poorly surfaced, water transport offered a smooth, fairly rapid ride from the railhead and steamers were introduced on the three largest lakes, Windermere, Coniston and Ullswater. Before the steamers, passengers could travel under sail and oar, and cargo was certainly moved by barges, again sail and oar. But steam power offered reliability. In 1845 the paddler *Lady of the Lake* was put into commission on Windermere, two years before the opening of the railway from Kendal to Windermere. Real progress came with the arrival of the Furness Railway Lakeside branch from Ulverston in 1869, and the final acquisition of the Windermere steamer fleet by the Furness in 1872. They embarked on a fairly ambitious expansion programme starting with the *Swan,* ordered in 1869. She set the fashion for the future, a twin screw vessel with a canoe shaped bow and overhanging counter stern. She and her sisters were all called yachts, because white painted they looked like yachts, and the tradition has persisted.

On Coniston the Coniston Railway Company ordered a steamer in 1859, the famous *Gondola* which the National Trust have rescued and restored. She carried all the traffic until the arrival of the *Lady of the Lake* in 1908. On Ullswater sailings also started in 1859, with a steamer called the *Enterprise,* but two larger vessels appeared in 1877 and 1889, the *Lady of the Lake* and the *Raven,* both still in service, but diesel powered. Quite a different *Raven* was the Furness Railway cargo steamer on Windermere, built in 1871. She delivered coal and goods up and down the Lake from the Lakeside railhead and is now preserved at the Windermere Steamboat Museum.

Top of page: Launch of the *Dragon Fly* with a full head of steam at Low Wood near Ambleside in 1850. She was built for the Windermere Iron Steam Boat Company with a double ended hull like a Mersey ferry of the period. (Illustrated London News. *Cumbria County Libraries, Kendal.*)

Bottom of page: Setting the fashion for Windermere's steamers, the first *Swan* of 1869 built by T. B. Seath of Rutherglen on the Clyde for the Windermere United Steam Yacht Company, taken over by the Furness Railway in 1872. The *Swan* lasted until 1938 when she was replaced by the present motor vessel of the same name. (*Raymond Sankey.*)

Running mate of the first *Swan* was the first *Teal*, steel built in 1879 by the Barrow Shipbuilding Company. She lasted until 1927. Behind her in this Bowness scene is the Furness Railway's cargo steamer *Raven,* Seath built in 1871, and now on show at the Windermere Steamboat Museum. *(Cumbria County Libraries, Kendal.)*

The *Tern* built in 1891 leaving Ambleside packed to capacity. Her engines were non condensing, so she used to puff like a locomotive, but in muted tones. *(Cumbria County Libraries, Kendal.)*

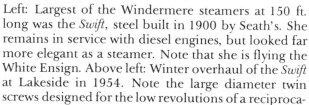

Left: Largest of the Windermere steamers at 150 ft. long was the *Swift*, steel built in 1900 by Seath's. She remains in service with diesel engines, but looked far more elegant as a steamer. Note that she is flying the White Ensign. Above left: Winter overhaul of the *Swift* at Lakeside in 1954. Note the large diameter twin screws designed for the low revolutions of a reciproca-tion steam engine. The Lakeside signalbox is to the right. And above right: The engineer of the *Swift* beside the controls of the two compound engines. Behind him is the smokebox of the locomotive type boiler. *(Cumbria County Libraries, Kendal; Author; John Garbutt.)*

Top left: Now restored after many decades of idleness the *Gondola* was Coniston's steamer from 1859 to 1908 when she became reserve vessel to the new *Lady of the Lake*. The *Gondola* was built on the Mersey by Jones Quiggin & Co., famous for the blockade runners they launched during the American Civil War. Sold in 1944 she remained moored as a house-boat at the foot of Coniston Lake until rescued by the National Trust in 1978. She is now back in service. *(Raymond Sankey.)*

Bottom left: Assembled at Waterhead, Coniston, by Thornycroft's, the *Lady of the Lake* was launched in 1908. Much larger than the *Gondola,* she did the bulk of the work until withdrawal from service in 1939. She remained laid up until scrapped in 1950. The photograph shows launching day for the *Lady of the Lake.* Her design followed Windermere practice, the canoe bow and counter stern. *(Raymond Sankey.)*

Below: Ullswater has two passenger vessels, the *Lady of the Lake* and the *Raven* both iron, built by Seath's in 1877 and 1889 respectively. Both were dieselized in 1934/5. The *Raven*, here seen off Howtown in her steam days, has had continuous service except for the war years, but the *Lady of the Lake* has just (1979) re-entered service, having been damaged by fire in 1965 and subsequently laid up. *(Ullswater Navigation & Transit Co. Ltd.)*

Ferries

North-West England is not pierced by wide rivers or long arms of the sea like the West Highlands, so ferries are not numerous. Windermere had rowing ferries of some sort from time immemorial both across and up and down the lake. Today that across the lake from Sawrey to Cockshot Point below Bowness remains, the oared barge giving way to a steam cable worked ferry in 1870, the barge remaining in reserve until the 1930s. The wire cable was wound one turn round a pulley driven by the steam engine. A bigger steam ferry was commissioned in 1915 and a bigger again in 1954. This is the *Drake* dieselized in 1960.

The other ferries worked in a different setting. That between Walney and Barrow Island was a chain worked steamer placed in service in 1878, replaced by a larger vessel in 1902, which lasted until 1908 when the bridge was opened. They were larger editions of the Winder-mere vessels. But there was also a battery electric ferry between the shipyard and Vickerstown which ran for a few years in the early 1900s.

Finally the Fleetwood–Knott End ferry started with sail and oar in 1841 and was converted to steam in 1893. Today the neat steamers have been replaced by motor vessels but they do not take vehicles, so Knott End remains difficult of access by road.

Top of page: Fleetwood–Knott End twin screw ferry *Wyresdale* built in 1925 by James Robertson & Sons (Fleetwood) Ltd. She was coal fired with twin compound engines. After a tragic boiler explosion in 1957, in which three men were killed, she was scrapped. The service is now maintained by the motor vessel *Viking 66*. (*Raymond Sankey.*)

Top left: Second of the Windermere steam ferries built in 1915 and replaced in 1954 by the present *Drake* now dieselized. *(Raymond Sankey.)*

Bottom left: Able to carry many hundreds of shipyard workers and a score of vehicles, this Walney steam chain ferry was put into service in 1902, replacing a smaller one, but she herself became redundant when the bridge was opened in 1908. *(Raymond Sankey.)*

Below: Battery powered electric ferry used from 1903 to take workers from the shipyard to South Vickerstown for their dinner. The electric ferry was named .the *Mudlark,* measuring 50 ft. long and capable of 5 knots. She could carry 240 passengers, but no vehicles. *(Cumbria County Libraries, Barrow-in-Furness.)*

Yachts

ESPERANCE in her steam days. It would be wonderful if her steam plant could be returned to her, doubtless the eventual aim of the Windermere Steamboat Museum.

There were sailing yachts on Windermere in the eighteenth century but steam yachts were scarce until the latter half of the nineteenth. Some very elaborate ones were built in those days of great wealth and ostentation, one or two almost of sea-going standard. Best known is the *Esperance* now preserved at the Windermere Steamboat Museum. She was built in 1869 by T. B. Seath of Rutherglen on the upper Clyde for H. W. Schneider, the Barrow ironmaster, on canoe lines like Coniston's *Gondola*. More conventional in appearance was the much larger *Britannia* built in 1879 also by Seath for Colonel G. J. M. Ridehalgh. The Furness Railway bought her in 1907 and turned her into a directors' yacht. She was perhaps the most handsome steamer ever on Lake Windermere.

Steam yachts with sleeping accommodation and galleys were for the really wealthy, but their scope on Windermere was limited. More popular and more numerous were the steam launches which came in all sizes from 15 feet up to 50 or more. A very good cross section of them are preserved at the Steamboat Museum. Some were simple work boats, for running around the Lake and for fishing. Others had small saloons and toilet facilities, and were used for elaborate Edwardian picnics. A steam coil from the boiler heated a tea urn with rapid efficiency.

Few sea-going steam yachts were based on the area, the only one of note was Sir James Ramsden's *Aries* built at Barrow in 1873.

Left: Sir James Ramsden's yacht *Aries* was an early product of the Barrow Shipbuilding Company founded in 1871 but struggling for orders. A yacht for the founder was one way to give employment and the *Aries* was launched in 1873, the first vessel to leave the ways at the new yard. This *Aries* seems to have sunk off Holyhead in 1880, certainly there was a second *Aries* built in 1881 for Sir James Ramsden. A half model of one of these yachts is in the collection of Merseyside County Museums. *(Vickers Shipbuilding Group Ltd.)*

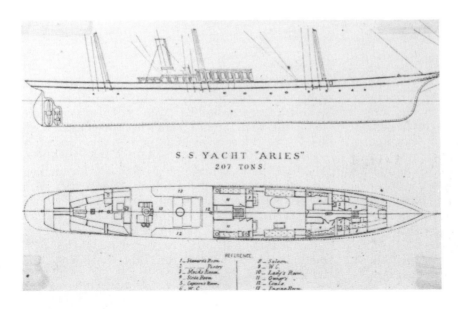

S.S. YACHT "ARIES"
207 TONS

Top left: One of the best known of the Windermere steam launches; the twin screw *Esperance,* iron built in 1869 by T. B. Seath of Rutherglen for H. W. Schneider the Barrow ironmaster, who lived at Belsfield, Bowness. He needed a steam launch to catch his train for Barrow at Lakeside. It was an early morning special, before the scheduled services started. The *Esperance* is now preserved at the Windermere Steamboat Museum, although her steam plant has long been replaced by two petrol engines. *(Raymond Sankey.)*

Bottom left: Largest of all the private vessels on Windermere, the *Britannia* was iron built in 1879 by Scath's of Rutherglen for Colonel G. J. M. Ridehalgh of Fellfoot. She was 107 ft. long and magnificently appointed. In 1907 the Furness Railway bought her as a directors' yacht, but she was scrapped in 1919. This picture shows her in F. R. days flying the White Ensign and the company's house flag at the main. *(Raymond Sankey.)*

Left: Now the oldest mechanically propelled vessel in the world, the *Dolly* was built about 1850 on Windermere. She spent some of her working life on Ullswater where she sank in the great frost of 1895. In 1962 she was raised and returned to Windermere for restoration, although hull, boiler and engine were found to be in perfect condition after their long immersion. She is now regularly steamed on Windermere, admittedly with a new boiler, recently installed, and may be seen at the Windermere Steamboat Museum. *(Windermere Steamboat Museum.)*

Left: Faster than most steam launches the steel hulled *Otto* was built in 1896 by Forrest & Sons, Wyvenhoe, Essex, builders of the *Tern*. She has a Sisson triple expansion engine and is capable of 18 mph. Some launches were built as speedboats, for example the *Satanella* with a quadruple expansion engine which drove her at 23 mph. Her boiler burnt 40 gallons of paraffin an hour. *(Windermere Steamboat Museum.)*

Right: Most opulent of the preserved launches at the Windermere Steamboat Museum is the *Branksome* built in 1891 by Brockbank's of Windermere for Mrs Howarth of Langdale Chase. Mr George Pattinson, founder of the museum, eventually acquired her and she is very frequently in steam. Her compound engine is by Sisson's of Gloucester, one of the last builders of steam marine engines in the British Isles. *(Windermere Steamboat Museum.)*

Top: Typical of the many steam launches which there used to be on Windermere the *Swallow* was built in 1911 by Shepherd's at Bowness. She has a Sisson triple expansion engine. Some launches were converted to motor and a few ex-steamers still ply for hire on the Lake, magnificently built and because of their limitation to fresh water, exceptionally long lived. (*Windermere Steamboat Museum.*)

Bottom: Smallest of the steam exhibits at the Windermere Steamboat Museum is the 18 ft. wooden hulled *Lady Elizabeth* dating from 1895. She has a single cylinder engine and a paraffin fired water tube boiler. Her quietness makes her ideal for char fishing, trolling with 90 ft. long lines for this deep water fish. (*Windermere Steamboat Museum.*)

Shipbuilding

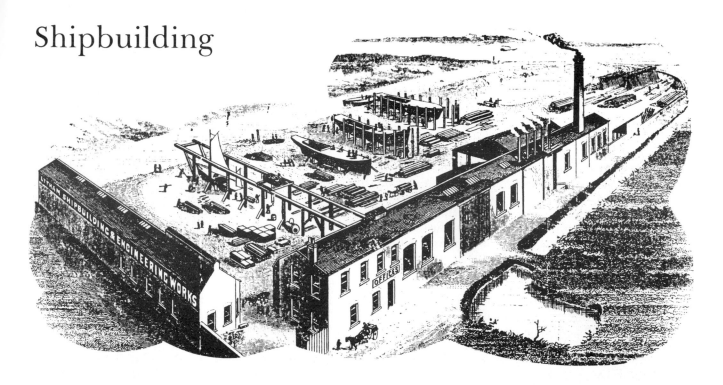

Still a major industry in the north west, but now concentrated into one huge centre, Barrow-in-Furness, shipbuilding in the nineteenth century was very widespread, from Maryport to Preston. The changes from sail to steam and from wooden to iron hulls meant a shipbuilding revolution. The little old yards at Greenodd, Ulverston and in the Duddon could not finance the construction of iron steamships. They relied on local timber and when the wooden sailing ship died, they died. The new yards grew up near centres of iron and coal production. Thus at Maryport the famous and long lived Ritson yard was founded in the 1830s and lasted until 1902 when it was taken over by other interests. Closure of the yard in 1914 helped to leave 80 per cent of Maryport without work.

Workington was an equally busy shipbuilding centre, both ports turning out large steel sailing ships as well as steamers, among the last British yards to build windjammers. R. Williamson was the great name at Workington, starting at Harrington in 1834 and moving to Workington in 1879 where ships were built under cover. Williamson's closed down in 1938. At Whitehaven, The Whitehaven Shipbuilding Company were in business from 1869 to 1891 as shipbuilders, but continued with repairs, the last of a long line of Whitehaven shipyards.

Top of page: Detail from an early brochure of the Lytham Shipbuilding and Engineering Company. *(Keith Ingham.)*

Barrow-in-Furness was a comparative latecomer to iron shipbuilding. The old Ashburner yard built wooden schooners from 1847 to 1883, but the modern industry was founded in 1871 by Sir James Ramsden. This was the Barrow Shipbuilding Company which in 1872 was employing 600 men. Four ships were projected for a Barrow based steamship company which was to bring jute from Calcutta to the new mills in the town. But this venture did not materialise and the Shipbuilding Company later ran into financial difficulties, although they built extensively for the Admiralty and for the Anchor line, and finally in 1881 the large liner the *City of Rome* for the Inman Line of Liverpool. But the company were dissatisfied with her and returned her to the builders. She ended up under the Anchor Line flag. By the mid 1880s orders for the shipyard were declining, yet salvation came from the submarine designer Nordenfeldt who was looking for a yard to develop his ideas. Warship building seemed to hold out a greater prospect for Barrow and in 1888 a new shipbuilding company was formed, the Naval Construction and Armaments Company. They did build merchant ships, but concentrated more and more on warships, completing in 1896 H.M.S. *Powerful*, the largest cruiser in the world.

For this reason the yard was attractive to the expanding Vickers organization who took over in 1896–7 and turned the venture into one of the largest naval shipbuilding yards in the world. They have built for the world's navies, notably Japan, completing the *Mikasa* in 1901, flagship of the fleet which defeated the Russians at Tsu-shima, and for South America. Amalgamation with Armstrongs of Elswick on the Tyne came in 1927 as a measure of rationalization, and the new firm Vickers-Armstrongs weathered the depression, securing orders for large passenger liners from P. & O. and others. But the accent was always on warships and in particular on submarines. To-day Vickers, a part of British Shipbuilders, are the country's leading submarine builders, with a wealth of expertise and tradition back to the days of Nordenfeldt.

South of Barrow there were shipyards at Glasson Dock, Lancaster, Preston and Lytham. At Glasson Dock Nicholson and Simpson were founded in the late 1830s and built many schooners. The Nicholsons remained in business as ship repairers until the 1960s. The Lancaster yard was primarily interested in sailing ships but at Preston W. Allsupp & Sons, in business between 1865 and 1904, built small iron steamers, ferries for the Mersey and iron horse-drawn boats for the Lancaster Canal. Another Preston yard, Richard Smith, founded in the 1870s who built iron steam tugs for the Bridgewater Canal, moved in about 1890 to Lytham, because of the height restrictions of the new Penwortham road bridge. From 1905 they called themselves the Lytham Shipbuilding and Engineering Co. Ltd., specializing in shallow draught river steamers for the colonies. Their last job was the steam cable ferry *Drake* for Windermere in 1954.

Lakes boatbuilding flourished during the nineteenth century, Borwick's of Bowness being an early establishment. They built steam launches as did Shepherd's and Brockbank's. Larger vessels for lake use were built elsewhere and sent to Windermere, Coniston and Ullswater in sections for assembly on the shore. Many came from T. B. Seath of Rutherglen, above Glasgow, specialists in small passenger steamers.

All launches at Maryport were broadside into the narrow Ellen. Ritson's were the biggest yard, although they sold out in 1902. Their last ship was the coaster *Lycidas*, top, launched in that year. The coaster *Point Clear* bottom, was launched by Ritson's in 1901. *(Both photographs Miss Annie Robinson, Maryport Maritime Museum.)*

Built by R. Williamson & Son of Workington in 1901, the *Horn*, 641 gross tons, was delivered to German owners but came under the British flag after the 1914–18 War, registered at Goole. She was a typical British designed, engines aft coaster. *(Whitehaven Museum.)*

Top left: Barrow shipyard in the early days of the Barrow Shipbuilding Company with a merchant steamer fitting out in the Devonshire Dock berth. *(Watercolour in the collection of the Furness Museum.)*

Bottom left: Fitting out in Devonshire Dock, Barrow, the light cruiser *Juno*, launched in November 1895. She had eleven 6 inch and 4.7 guns, mostly mounted for broadside fire. *(Vickers Shipbuilding Group Ltd.)*

The largest cruiser in the world, H.M.S. *Powerful* launched by the Naval Construction and Armaments Company at Barrow in 1895. At that date she was the biggest warship they had so far built and showed the Admiralty what Barrow shipwrights and engineers were capable of achieving. *(N. Coulton.)*

Completed at Vickers, Barrow-in-Furness in November 1960 the *Oriana* leaves for her trials. For her it was a narrow squeeze through the Ramsden dock entrance lock. Built for the P. & O.–Orient Line the *Oriana* (40,340 gross tons) was the last of four post war Orient passenger liners ordered from Vickers and is still in service as a cruise ship. *(Author.)*

Bibliography

Burtt, Frank.	Cross Channel and Coastal Paddle Steamers. Richard Tilling, 1934.
Duckworth, C. L. D. & Langmuir, G. E.	Railway and Other Steamers. T. Stephenson & Sons Ltd., Prescot, 1968. (2 ed).
Henry, Fred.	Ships of the Isle of Man Steam Packet Co. Ltd. Brown, Son & Ferguson Ltd., Glasgow, 1967. (2 ed).
McNeill, D. B.	Irish Passenger Steamship Services. Vols 1 & 2. David & Charles, Newton Abbot, 1969.
Moore, A. W.	The Historical Account of the Isle of Man Steam Packet Co., 1904.
Waine, Charles V.	Steam Coasters and Short Sea Traders. Waine Research Publications, Albrighton, 1976.

Also Sea Breezes, Ships Monthly (periodicals), many useful references, and two excellent museum publications.

McNeill, D. B.	Coastal Passenger Steamers and Inland Navigations in the North of Ireland. (No. 3. Transport Handbook).
Pearsall, A. W. H.	Coastal Passenger Steamers of Southern Ireland. (No. 6. Transport Handbook).

Both from the Ulster Museum, Belfast.

Leaving Silloth, a steam coaster riding light. *(Malcolm Wilson.)*

COUNTRYSIDE PUBLICATIONS LIMITED

CURRENT BOOK AND PRICE LIST

* LARGE FORMAT (A4) BOOKS 'IN TIMES PAST' SERIES

- ☐ STOCKTON (ISBN 0 86157 015 4: 44 pps; 62 photographs); £1.50
- ☐ LANCASTER & MORECAMBE (ISBN 0 86157 004 9: 40 pps; 74 photographs): £1.65
- ☐ STRETFORD (ISBN 0 86157 024 3: 40 pps; 62 photographs): £1.60
- ☐ GATESHEAD (ISBN 0 86157 026 X: 48 pps; 71 photographs): £1.80

* SMALL FORMAT (A5) BOOKS 'IN TIMES PAST' SERIES

- ☐ WORKSOP (ISBN 0 86157 023 5: 48 pps; 59 photographs): £1.20
- ☐ HEATHROW & DISTRICT (ISBN 0 86157 014 6: 64 pps; 71 photographs): £1.50
- ☐ BOOTLE (ISBN 0 86157 022 7: 40 pps; 41 photographs): £1.20
- ☐ LYTHAM ST. ANNE'S (ISBN 0 86157 010 3: 56 pps; 64 photographs): £1.25
- ☐ SUTTON IN ASHFIELD (ISBN 0 86157 006 5: 48 pps; 56 photographs): £1.00
- ☐ ULVERSTON (ISBN 0 86157 020 0: 48 pps; 54 photographs): £1.20
- ☐ THIRSK PAST AND PRESENT (ISBN 0 86157 029 4: 48 pps; 49 photographs): £1.45

* SMALL FORMAT (A5) SPECIALIZED RECIPE BOOKS

- ☐ LANCASHIRE RECIPES OLD & NEW (ISBN 0 86157 018 9: 48 pps; 85 recipes; 19 vintage illustrations): £1.00
- ☐ LAKELAND RECIPES OLD & NEW (ISBN 0 86157 008 1: 80 pps; 123 recipes; 21 vintage illustrations): £1.50
- ☐ GLOUCESTERSHIRE RECIPES OLD & NEW (ISBN 0 86157 013 8: 48 pps; 100 recipes; 15 vintage illustrations): £1.00
- ☐ GAME COOKERY – SOFT BACK (ISBN 0 86157 035 9: 120 pps selected WAGBI approved recipes; Menus; Cordon Bleu freezer section): £1.90

* MISCELLANEOUS SMALL FORMAT BOOKS

- ☐ EXPLORING HISTORIC CUMBRIA (ISBN 0 86157 005 7: 48 pps; 32 photographs): £1.25
- ☐ OVER THE SETTS (ISBN 0 86157 007 3: 48 pps; 43 vintage photographs of East Lancashire trams and buses in days gone by): £1.00
- ☐ WILLIAM FOGGITT'S WEATHER BOOK (ISBN 0 86157 012 X: 64 pps; 18 photographs; 7 line subjects; monthly weather lore): £1.00

- ☐ RIBBLE VALLEY RENDEZVOUS (ISBN 0 86157 011 1: 48 pps; 29 photographs; Where to Go; Where to Dine; What to See; An illustrated itinerary): £1.20
- ☐ SMILIN' THROUGH (ISBN 0 86157 036 7: 48 pps. A collection of Lancashire Dialect poetry. 11 illustrations by Bill Tidy): Soft back £1.80; Hard back £3.20
- ☐ BARROW AT WAR (ISBN 0 86157 027 8: 48 pps): £1.20
- ☐ WINDOW ON WHALLEY (ISBN 0 86157 019 7: 32 pps; 14 photographs): £1.00
- ☐ NEWARK-ON-TRENT (ISBN 0 86157 030 8: 48 pps; 46 photographs): £1.45
- ☐ LANGBAURGH (ISBN 0 86157 033 2: 48 pps): **£1.80**
- ☐ STOURBRIDGE (ISBN 0 86157 045 6: 48 pps): **£2.00**
- ☐ KIDDERMINSTER (ISBN 0 86157 037 5: 48 pps): **£1.80**
- ☐ RUNCORN (ISBN 0 86157 032 4: 48 pps): **£1.80**

* OTHER COUNTRYSIDE PUBLICATIONS

- ☐ NORTH WESTERN SAIL (Large A4 format: ISBN 0 86157 002 2: 56 pps; 112 photographs; from Whitehaven to Blackpool); £1.85

All the above publications are in print, and should normally be available through your bookseller or larger newsagent. In case of difficulty, however, please direct your requirements to:
COUNTRYSIDE PUBLICATIONS LIMITED, SCHOOL LANE, BRINSCALL, Nr. CHORLEY, LANCASHIRE, ENGLAND, remitting the stated amount by cheque or postal order.

> * SPECIALITY BOOKS (SEE OVERLEAF)

COUNTRYSIDE PUBLICATIONS LIMITED

THE FATE OF THE LANCASHIRE WITCHES

In 1612, the English county of Lancaster was infested with an outbreak of witchcraft on a hitherto unprecedented scale – so much so that local magistrate and landowner Roger Nowell determined on a course of action which was to inflame passions to a degree that reached as far north as Lancaster Castle and as far south as the palace of King James.

In his book *The Fate of the Lancashire Witches*, Arthur Douglas has adopted a style which presents these compelling events in a new and dramatic way – that of isolating each of the historical pivots upon which the drama turns and projecting it into the present tense, a technique that at once creates an authenticity of atmosphere and characterization. Each such episode is followed by an orthodox narrative in which the motives and by an orthodox narrative in which the motives and actions of those taking part are examined and commented upon.

Taken together, these diverse yet complementary elements of the book breath new life into the long-dead bones of Old Mother Demdike, Chattox, Alice Nutter and the rest; cast fresh light on the actions of Roger Nowell and his fellow magistrates; open wide the sealed doors and shuttered windows masking the so-called art and practice of witchcraft in seventeenth-century England. . . .

THE FATE OF THE LANCASHIRE WITCHES (ISBN 0 86157 001 4: small A5 format; 48 pps; 17 photographs; 8 interpretive line and wash drawings; witches' family tree; centre-spread map of Lancashire Witchways; four-colour front cover): **£1.25**
Also available in hard-back version (ISBN 0 86157 041 3): **£2.60**

SPECIALITY PRODUCTIONS

WILL THE REAL JACK THE RIPPER . . .

In the autumn of 1888, the East End of London was visited with a series of murders so horrendous in their concept and execution that even the denizens of Whitechapel were jolted into such expressions of fear and outrage that the authorities feared for the safety of the Realm itself.

One by one the pitiful victims fell to the bloody knife of Jack the Ripper; one by one those suspected of the crimes were arrested; and one by one they were released. The rampage of the Ripper ran for nine weeks and a day – from the early morning of Friday the 31st of August to that of Friday the 9th of November – and in that duration the unknown killer struck five times, until finally, with the events of the 9th of November, he reached his climactic, never to kill again. Or did he?

In his reconstruction *Will the Real Jack the Ripper . . .* Arthur Douglas takes each episodic element of the case and presents it starkly and factually in the present tense. Each such episode is followed by an analysis of the subsequent investigation, a process that leads, if not to a solution to the Ripper riddle, to a critical look at the evidence and the interpretation placed upon it, and, in one case at least, to the consideration of a new possibility. The outcome is dramatic, thought-provoking reading for all *Ripperologists*.

WILL THE REAL JACK THE RIPPER . . . (ISBN 0 86157 025 1: A5 format; 72 pps; photographs; interpretive line drawings; library map of murder sites; satirical cartoons; two-colour front cover): **£1.60**
Also available in hard-back version: **£3.20**
